DEFINING MOMENTS IN CANADIAN HISTORY

The
BRITISH NORTH AMERICA ACT

Weigl

Published by Weigl Educational Publishers Limited
6325 10th Street S.E.
Calgary, AB T2H 2Z9
Website: www.weigl.com

All of the Internet URLs given in the book were valid at the time of publication.
However, due to the dynamic nature of the Internet, some addresses may have changed,
or sites may have ceased to exist since publication. While the author and publisher
regret any inconvenience this may cause readers, no responsibility for any such
changes can be accepted by either the author or the publisher.

Library and Archives Canada Cataloguing-in-Publication Data available upon request.
Fax (403) 233-7769 for the attention of the Publishing Records department.

ISBN 978-1-77071-614-8

Printed in the United States of America in North Mankato, Minnesota
1 2 3 4 5 6 7 8 9 0 14 13 12 11 10

072010
WEP230610

Project Coordinator: Heather C. Hudak
Author: Penny Dowdy
Editor: Bill Becker

Every reasonable effort has been made to trace ownership and to obtain permission
to reprint copyright material. The publishers would be pleased to have any errors or
omissions brought to their attention so that they may be corrected in
subsequent printings.

We gratefully acknowledge the financial support of the Government of Canada through
the Canada Book Fund for our publishing activities.

Contents

Overview   **Page 4**

The British North   **Pages 6–29**
America Act

Brain Teasers   **Page 30**

Further Information   **Page 31**

Glossary/Index   **Page 32**

Overview

People from Europe in the 17th and 18th centuries explored the land that is now known as Canada. Great Britain and France claimed land as colonies. After the Seven Years' War, France gave up its claim to much of the land that it held to Great Britain. The British governed the colonies for more than 100 years. Some colonies continued to practise their French culture and traditions while under French control.

Both the British government and people living in the colonies had reason to make the Canadian colonies **independent**. The **colonists** wanted to control their own government. Great Britain could save money by letting the people in the colonies pay for their own government and protection. In 1867, the Parliament of Great Britain approved the British North America Act. The act gave Canada its independence and established Canada's first **constitution**.

Background Information

Sir John A. Macdonald - John A. McDonald was a politician who worked for Canadian independence from Great Britain. He became Canada's first prime minister.

George-Étienne Cartier - George-Étienne Cartier was a politician from Quebec who worked for Canada's independence. Cartier served as a member of the Parliament of Canada and the Legislature of Quebec.

Thomas D'Arcy McGee - Thomas D'Arcy McGee was a newspaper editor and politician in Quebec who supported Canadian independence. He served in the first Parliament of Canada.

Charles Tupper - Charles Tupper was a politician who supported Canada's independence. Tupper was Canada's sixth prime minister.

George Brown - George Brown founded the *Toronto Globe* newspaper and supported the Underground Railroad that provided safe passage to escaped slaves from the United States. Brown rallied French Canadians to support an independent Canada.

Legend:
- France
- Great Britain
- Territories ceded by France to Great Britain by the Treaty of Utrecht in 1713
- Spain

Hudson Bay

CANADA

Newfoundland

Upper Country

Quebec (1608)

ACADIA

Boston (1630)

New York (1626)
Philadelphia (1681)

Upper Louisiana (Illinois Country)

Pacific Ocean

Atlantic Ocean

LOUISIANA

Lower Louisiana

Gulf of Mexico

IN THE 1700S, EUROPEAN EXPLORERS RACED TO CREATE **SETTLEMENTS** IN UNEXPLORED AREAS AND EXPAND THEIR EMPIRES. FRENCH EXPLORERS TRAVELLED ALONG THE ST. LAWRENCE RIVER AND EVENTUALLY FOUNDED THE COLONIES THAT BECAME NEW FRANCE.

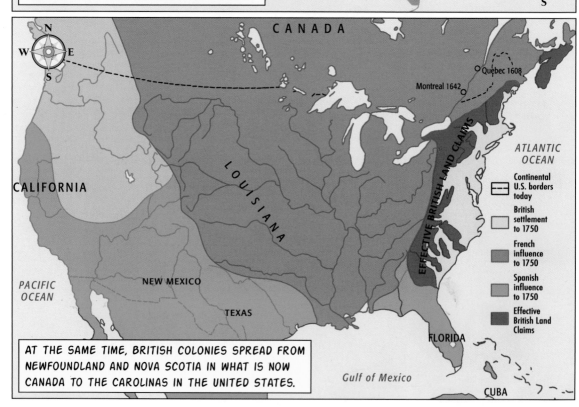

CANADA

Quebec 1608

Montreal 1642

ATLANTIC OCEAN

CALIFORNIA

L O U I S I A N A

EFFECTIVE BRITISH LAND CLAIMS

Legend:
- Continental U.S. borders today
- British settlement to 1750
- French influence to 1750
- Spanish influence to 1750
- Effective British Land Claims

PACIFIC OCEAN

NEW MEXICO

TEXAS

FLORIDA

Gulf of Mexico

CUBA

AT THE SAME TIME, BRITISH COLONIES SPREAD FROM NEWFOUNDLAND AND NOVA SCOTIA IN WHAT IS NOW CANADA TO THE CAROLINAS IN THE UNITED STATES.

The Seven Years' War was fought by nearly every major European power. In North America, the battles were primarily between the French and British. The two countries were trying to take control of each other's holdings.

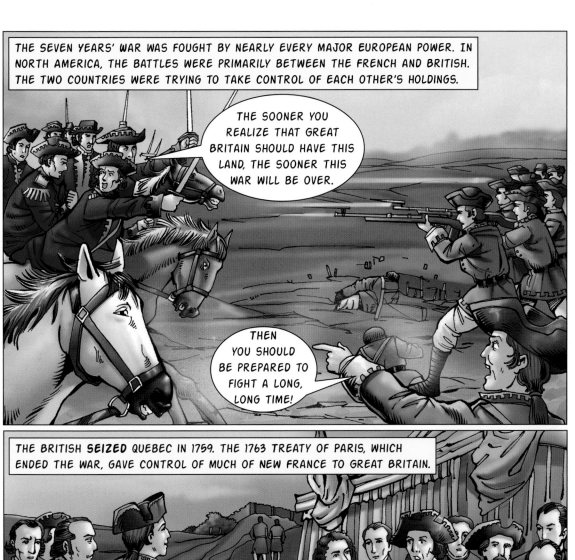

The British **seized** Quebec in 1759. The 1763 Treaty of Paris, which ended the war, gave control of much of New France to Great Britain.

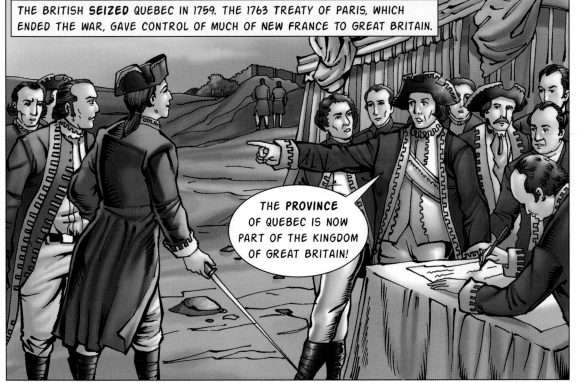

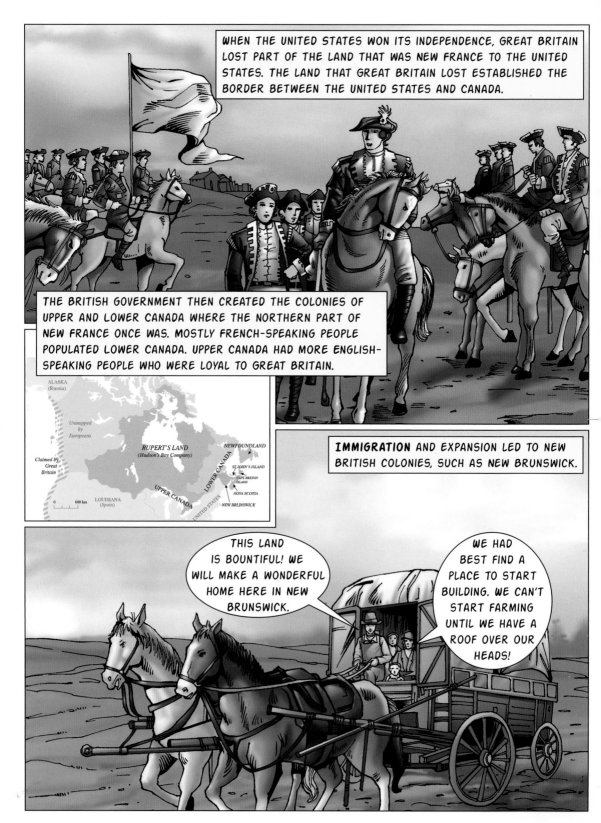

WHEN THE UNITED STATES WON ITS INDEPENDENCE, GREAT BRITAIN LOST PART OF THE LAND THAT WAS NEW FRANCE TO THE UNITED STATES. THE LAND THAT GREAT BRITAIN LOST ESTABLISHED THE BORDER BETWEEN THE UNITED STATES AND CANADA.

THE BRITISH GOVERNMENT THEN CREATED THE COLONIES OF UPPER AND LOWER CANADA WHERE THE NORTHERN PART OF NEW FRANCE ONCE WAS. MOSTLY FRENCH-SPEAKING PEOPLE POPULATED LOWER CANADA. UPPER CANADA HAD MORE ENGLISH-SPEAKING PEOPLE WHO WERE LOYAL TO GREAT BRITAIN.

IMMIGRATION AND EXPANSION LED TO NEW BRITISH COLONIES, SUCH AS NEW BRUNSWICK.

THIS LAND IS BOUNTIFUL! WE WILL MAKE A WONDERFUL HOME HERE IN NEW BRUNSWICK.

WE HAD BEST FIND A PLACE TO START BUILDING. WE CAN'T START FARMING UNTIL WE HAVE A ROOF OVER OUR HEADS!

IN UPPER CANADA, BRITISH COLONISTS UPHELD THE LAWS OF GREAT BRITAIN. THESE COLONISTS ALSO WORSHIPED IN CHURCHES SIMILAR TO THE ONES THEY HAD IN GREAT BRITAIN.

THIS IS SUCH A WONDERFUL OPPORTUNITY. WE NEVER WOULD HAVE BEEN ABLE TO OWN THIS MUCH LAND BACK IN LONDON.

LOWER CANADA RETAINED THE LANGUAGE, LAWS, AND CULTURE OF NEW FRANCE. MANY FRENCH CANADIANS RESENTED BRITISH RULE. SOME PEOPLE IN LOWER CANADA TRIED TO **REBEL** AGAINST BRITISH AUTHORITY, BUT THEY WERE DEFEATED BY THE BRITISH MILITARY.

I HAVE HEARD RUMOURS OF A REBELLION. I WANT TO HELP.

YES, WE CAN'T KEEP LIVING AS IF WE WERE BRITISH. THEY HAVE NO RESPECT FOR OUR RELIGION OR OUR TRADITIONS!

IT'S TOO RISKY. SOME OF THE MEN OUTSIDE OF TOWN ATTACKED THE BRITISH FORT LAST NIGHT. THE BRITISH HAVE TOO MANY WEAPONS. WE CAN'T WIN.

MAINTAINING A GOVERNMENT IN EACH BRITISH COLONY COST GREAT BRITAIN A GREAT DEAL OF MONEY.

PLEASE SEND WORD BACK TO THE KING AS SOON AS POSSIBLE. WITHOUT MORE FUNDS, I CAN'T PAY THE SOLDIERS WE NEED TO KEEP THE PEACE.

I DON'T THINK THE KING WILL SEND MORE MONEY. THE WAR WITH THE UNITED STATES HAS DEPLETED BRITISH FUNDS. WE'D BE BETTER OFF RAISING MONEY ON OUR OWN RIGHT HERE.

UNDER BRITISH RULE, EACH COLONY HAD DIFFERENT LAWS AND CUSTOMS.

HOW MANY BEAVER SKINS DO YOU WANT?

I CAN ONLY TAKE 10. THAT'S THE MOST THE LAW WILL LET ME BUY FROM ONE TRADER.

WHAT? I'VE NEVER HEARD OF SUCH A LAW!

THAT'S HOW WE DO THINGS HERE. IT GIVES MORE TRADERS A CHANCE TO MAKE MONEY. IT ALSO MAKES SURE YOU CAN'T CHARGE ME TOO MUCH FOR EACH HIDE. THERE WILL ALWAYS BE OTHER TRADERS WITH HIDES IF YOUR PRICE IS TOO HIGH.

IF GREAT BRITAIN COULD MAKE CANADA A **DOMINION**, THEN IT COULD ALLOW THE PEOPLE IN CANADA TO START TAKING ON THE RESPONSIBILITIES AND COST OF RUNNING THE GOVERNMENT.

THE PEOPLE IN THE CANADIAN COLONIES WILL RAISE THEIR OWN TAXES. THEY WILL HAVE TO PROTECT THEMSELVES, BUILD THEIR OWN HOSPITALS, AND BUILD THEIR OWN BRIDGES.

MAKING CANADA ONE DOMINION INSTEAD OF MANY COLONIES WOULD ALSO HELP KEEP THE PEACE IN THE FORMER NEW FRANCE. THE FRENCH CANADIANS WOULD NOT BE THE MAJORITY IN THE DOMINION, SO THERE WOULD BE LESS CHANCE OF ANOTHER REBELLION.

I HEARD MORE RUMOURS ABOUT BRITAIN LETTING CANADA GOVERN ITSELF.

I HEARD THEM, TOO. IT WOULD BE WONDERFUL TO HAVE THE SUPPORT OF THE OTHER COLONIES IN KEEPING PEACE HERE IN QUEBEC.

BETWEEN 1763 AND 1884, OFFICIALS WROTE FOUR DIFFERENT CONSTITUTIONS FOR THE COLONIES. THESE INCLUDED 1763'S ROYAL PROCLAMATION, THE 1774 QUEBEC ACT, THE CONSTITUTIONAL ACT OF 1791, AND THE UNION ACT OF 1841.

THESE CANADIAN COLONIES ARE DRAINING GREAT BRITAIN'S FUNDS. WE HAVE TO COME UP WITH A CONSTITUTION ON WHICH EVERYONE CAN AGREE.

THAT'S EASIER SAID THAN DONE. EACH COLONY HAS ITS OWN PRIORITIES.

COLONISTS STARTED OPENLY DISCUSSING THE CREATION OF A **FEDERATION**.

"...SHOULD THE COLONIES CHOOSE TO JOIN AS A FEDERATION, THE CITIZENS WOULD CERTAINLY PAY LESS IN TAXES. WE WOULD NO LONGER BE RESPONSIBLE FOR PAYING **TRIBUTE** TO THE BRITISH CROWN."

AN ARGUMENT FOR FEDERATION

COMING TO AN AGREEMENT THAT SUITED EACH PROVINCE WAS DIFFICULT. EACH PROVINCE HAD ITS OWN LAWS, CULTURE, AND ECONOMY THAT IT WANTED TO PROTECT.

THE PEOPLE OF LOWER CANADA WANT THEIR FRENCH TRADITIONS PROTECTED.

CERTAINLY, BUT THE PEOPLE IN THE OTHER COLONIES DON'T WANT TO BE FORCED TO ADOPT FRENCH CUSTOMS!

ONE SUPPORTER OF A UNIFIED COUNTRY WAS JOHN ALEXANDER MACDONALD. HE HAD SERVED AS A LAWYER WHEN PEOPLE IN UPPER AND LOWER CANADA REBELLED AGAINST BRITISH RULE.

THIS MAN FELT THAT THE BRITISH **MILITIA** WAS THREATENING HIS FAMILY. HE SIMPLY ACTED IN SELF-DEFENCE.

CASE DISMISSED!

AFTER THE FRENCH-CANADIAN REBELLIONS, UPPER AND LOWER CANADA WERE COMBINED TO CREATE THE PROVINCE OF CANADA. MACDONALD SERVED AS THE ENGLISH CANADIAN JOINT PREMIER OF THE PROVINCE ALONG WITH ÉTIENNE-PASCHAL TACHÉ, A FRENCH-CANADIAN LEADER.

THE POPULATION AROUND MONTREAL HAS GROWN CONSIDERABLY. WE NEED TO START PLANNING MORE ROADS IN THE AREA.

I AGREE. WE CAN GET WORKERS STARTED THIS SPRING.

MACDONALD THEN SPENT YEARS TRYING TO GET THE BRITISH COLONIES TO AGREE TO COME TOGETHER AS ONE UNIFIED GROUP. DELEGATES MET IN CHARLOTTETOWN, PRINCE EDWARD ISLAND, QUEBEC CITY, QUEBEC, AND LONDON, ENGLAND, TO SET RULES AND POLICIES WITH WHICH EACH PROVINCE COULD AGREE.

WE CAN ALL AGREE, THEN, THAT EACH COLONY CAN CREATE VOTING LAWS FOR LOCAL ELECTIONS. NOW, WHAT IS THE NEXT ISSUE TO RESOLVE?

ONCE THE PROVINCES HAD COME TO AGREEMENT, MACDONALD BROUGHT THE PROPOSAL TO PARLIAMENT IN GREAT BRITAIN IN 1867.

I HOPE WE CAN FINALLY GET OUR PROPOSED CONSTITUTION APPROVED.

ANOTHER SUPPORTER OF A UNIFIED CANADA WAS GEORGE-ÉTIENNE CARTIER. CARTIER WAS A FRENCH CANADIAN INVOLVED IN THE REBELLION IN LOWER CANADA.

FIGHT HARD, MEN! REMEMBER WHAT WE HAVE LOST!

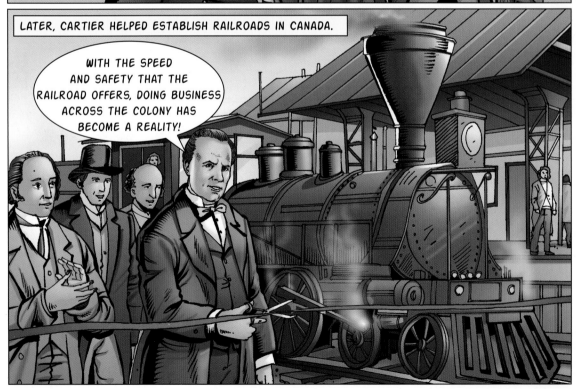

LATER, CARTIER HELPED ESTABLISH RAILROADS IN CANADA.

WITH THE SPEED AND SAFETY THAT THE RAILROAD OFFERS, DOING BUSINESS ACROSS THE COLONY HAS BECOME A REALITY!

CARTIER ALSO SERVED AS JOINT PREMIER OF THE PROVINCE OF CANADA WITH JOHN MACDONALD.

FORMER PREMIER TACHÉ SPEAKS VERY HIGHLY OF YOU, PREMIER MACDONALD.

PLEASE, CALL ME JOHN. I AM EAGER TO DISCUSS YOUR PLANS FOR EXPANDING THE RAILROAD IN CANADA.

CARTIER WAS CRITICAL IN GETTING THE SUPPORT OF FRENCH CANADIANS IN CREATING THE NEW FEDERATION. HE ALSO ATTENDED ALL THREE CONFERENCES IN CHARLOTTETOWN, QUEBEC, AND LONDON.

I ASSURE YOU THAT THE RIGHTS OF FRENCH-CANADIANS WILL BE PROTECTED IN ANY CONSTITUTION WE TAKE TO PARLIAMENT!

THOMAS D'ARCY MCGEE WAS A NEWSPAPER EDITOR BORN AND RAISED IN IRELAND. HE CAME TO CANADA TO START A NEWSPAPER CALLED THE *NEW ERA*.

STOP THE PRESSES! WE HAVE A NEW LEAD STORY!

MCGEE ALSO FOUGHT FOR THE RIGHTS OF IRISH IMMIGRANTS TO CANADIAN PROVINCES. HE WANTED TO ENSURE THEY COULD SERVE IN POLITICAL OFFICE AND PRACTISE THEIR CHOSEN RELIGION.

SIR, PLEASE READ THIS **PAMPHLET**. WE NEED TO LET OUR VOICES BE HEARD.

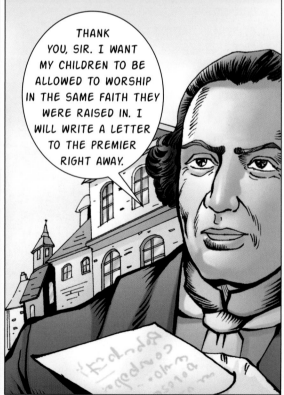

THANK YOU, SIR. I WANT MY CHILDREN TO BE ALLOWED TO WORSHIP IN THE SAME FAITH THEY WERE RAISED IN. I WILL WRITE A LETTER TO THE PREMIER RIGHT AWAY.

CHARLES TUPPER, ANOTHER SUPPORTER OF CANADIAN UNITY, WAS BORN IN NOVA SCOTIA AND TRAINED AS A DOCTOR.

I WILL COME BACK TOMORROW TO CHECK ON YOUR DAUGHTER MA'AM. PLEASE MAKE SURE SHE RESTS.

AS YOUR PREMIER, I AM SENDING MEDICAL AID TO THE COMMUNITIES THAT HAVE SUFFERED DURING THE LATEST INFLUENZA OUTBREAK.

ALONG WITH BEING A PHYSICIAN, TUPPER WAS A POLITICIAN. HE SERVED AS PREMIER OF NOVA SCOTIA.

LIKE THOMAS D'ARCY MCGEE, GEORGE BROWN WAS IN THE NEWSPAPER BUSINESS. HE MOVED FROM SCOTLAND TO NEW YORK AND THEN TO THE PROVINCE OF CANADA, WHERE HE RAN *THE GLOBE*.

"FACTORY WORKERS IN TORONTO CALL FOR SAFER WORKING CONDITIONS..."

BROWN EXPOSED THE CONDITIONS IN A PRISON IN CANADA. THIS LED HIM TO BECOME INVOLVED IN POLITICS.

SIR, WE DON'T HAVE CLEAN WATER. WE'RE LUCKY IF WE GET ONE MEAL A DAY.

I WILL MAKE SURE THAT EVERYONE KNOWS HOW OUR GOVERNMENT TREATS PRISONERS HERE.

BROWN HELPED SLAVES ESCAPE FROM THE SOUTHERN UNITED STATES AND WORKED TO KEEP SLAVERY OUT OF CANADA.

I CAN'T BELIEVE WE'RE FINALLY FREE. YOU'VE BEEN GREAT HELP TO ME AND MY FAMILY.

IT'S AN HONOUR FOR ME TO HELP. NO HUMAN SHOULD BE TREATED AS THE PROPERTY OF ANOTHER.

REPRESENTATIVES OF NOVA SCOTIA, NEW BRUNSWICK, CANADA, NEWFOUNDLAND, AND PRINCE EDWARD ISLAND SIGNED THE BRITISH NORTH AMERICA ACT, ALSO KNOWN AS THE BNA ACT. THE PROVINCE OF CANADA WOULD LATER BECOME THE TWO PROVINCES OF QUEBEC AND ONTARIO. THE REPRESENTATIVES HOPED THE BNA ACT WOULD SERVE AS THE CONSTITUTION FOR THE NEW COUNTRY.

GENTLEMEN, I BELIEVE WE HAVE A CONSTITUTION THAT EVERYONE WILL FIND ACCEPTABLE.

PRINCE EDWARD ISLAND AND NEWFOUNDLAND WOULD LATER REMOVE THEMSELVES FROM THE AGREEMENT.

WE DON'T BELIEVE THAT OUR COLONIES WILL BENEFIT FROM JOINING YOU AT THIS TIME.

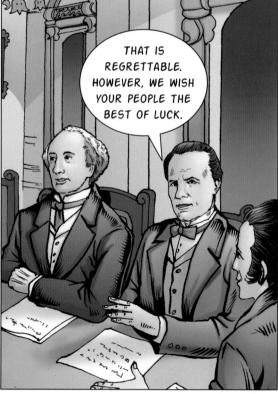

THAT IS REGRETTABLE. HOWEVER, WE WISH YOUR PEOPLE THE BEST OF LUCK.

MACDONALD AND BROWN BROUGHT THE BNA ACT TO THE BRITISH GOVERNMENT. THE LAWMAKERS IN GREAT BRITAIN WERE NOT PARTICULARLY INTERESTED IN HEARING THE MEN. ONLY 10 OF THE 400 MEMBERS OF THE BRITISH HOUSE WERE PRESENT FOR THE READING OF THE ACT.

AS LONG AS WE CAN GET THEM TO APPROVE THE BNA ACT, I DON'T CARE HOW MANY SHOW UP TO HEAR US READ THE ACT.

THIS CERTAINLY ISN'T A GREAT SHOW OF SUPPORT!

THERE WERE MANY SUGGESTIONS REGARDING NAMES FOR THE NEW COUNTRY. THE BRITISH HOUSE FINALLY DECIDED ON CANADA.

New Britain
Laurentia
Britanna
Acadia
Cabotia
Columbia
Canadia
Ursalia

ON 1 JULY, 1867, THE CONSTITUTION WENT INTO EFFECT. THE DOMINION OF CANADA WAS BORN.

Great Britain Signs the BNA Act "We are the Dominion of Canada"

INDEPENDENCE IS WONDERFUL!

OUR CHILDREN WILL GROW UP IN A **SOVEREIGN** NATION! HOORAY!

THE BNA ACT DIVIDED POWERS AND RESPONSIBILITIES BETWEEN THE PROVINCES AND THE NEW **FEDERAL** GOVERNMENT. THE FEDERAL GOVERNMENT WAS RESPONSIBLE FOR 29 AREAS OF RESPONSIBILITY. THESE INCLUDED TRADE, MILITARY AND DEFENCE, BANKING, AND IN GENERAL, KEEPING PEACE AND ORDER IN THE COUNTRY.

THE PROVINCES WERE RESPONSIBLE FOR LAWS RELATED TO PROPERTY, CIVIL RIGHTS, AND MAINTAINING HOSPITALS.

I WILL MISS TALKING TO YOU MRS. O'HARA. TODAY IS MY LAST DAY.

WHY ARE YOU LEAVING?

THE PROVINCE HAS BUILT A NEW HOSPITAL, AND THEY NEED NURSES THERE.

AT TIMES, IT WAS NOT CLEAR WHETHER AN ISSUE FELL UNDER PROVINCIAL OR FEDERAL LAW. THE CONSTITUTION SAID THAT IF THERE WAS A CONFLICT BETWEEN THE LAW OF A PROVINCE AND THE FEDERAL LAW, THE FEDERAL LAW WOULD RULE.

OUR PROVINCIAL LAW SAYS THAT THE LAND SHOULD BE AWARDED TO MR. ABBOTT'S BROTHER, THE CLOSEST MALE RELATIVE.

YOUR HONOUR, THE FEDERAL LAW SAYS THE WIDOW GETS ONE-THIRD OF THE ESTATE.

WE MUST FOLLOW THE FEDERAL LAW IN THIS CASE. MRS. ABBOTT RECEIVES ONE-THIRD OF THE ESTATE. THE BROTHER GETS THE REST.

TO THINK THAT THIS IS THE FIRST ELECTION IN WHICH I HAVE VOTED. THIS IS A REMARKABLE DAY.

NOW, MALE CANADIAN LANDOWNERS COULD VOTE FOR REPRESENTATIVES IN THEIR LEGISLATURE. EACH PROVINCE HAD ITS OWN LEGISLATURE.

27

FOR HIS PART IN HELPING CREATE THE DOMINION OF CANADA, QUEEN VICTORIA MADE MACDONALD A KNIGHT. A MONTH AFTER BRITISH PARLIAMENT APPROVED THE BNA, MACDONALD WAS ELECTED AS THE FIRST PRIME MINISTER OF THE DOMINION OF CANADA.

MACDONALD WANTED TO EXPAND AND UNIFY THE NEW COUNTRY. DURING HIS TIME IN OFFICE, CANADA BOUGHT LAND FROM THE HUDSON'S BAY COMPANY, A BRITISH COMPANY THAT WAS FORMED TO TRADE AND EXPLORE NORTH AMERICA. THE LAND PURCHASED FROM THE HUDSON'S BAY COMPANY BECAME THE PROVINCES OF MANITOBA AND BRITISH COLUMBIA, AS WELL AS THE NORTHWEST TERRITORIES. PRINCE EDWARD ISLAND ALSO AGREED TO JOIN CONFEDERATION.

MACDONALD PUSHED FOR A TRANSCONTINENTAL RAILROAD.

THIS RAILROAD WILL TAKE PEOPLE AND CARGO FROM THE ATLANTIC TO THE PACIFIC COASTS.

MACDONALD ALSO CALLED FOR THE CREATION OF THE ROYAL CANADIAN MOUNTED POLICE.

YOU ARE CHARGED WITH KEEPING THE CITIZENS OF CANADA SAFE.

Brain Teasers

1. How did the French parts of North America come under British control?

2. Who lived in Upper and Lower Canada?

3. Why did Great Britain consider giving up control of the North American colonies?

4. Why were creating a new country and building the railroad so closely related?

5. Which of the Founding Fathers became the first prime minister of Canada?

6. What did Macdonald accomplish after the Dominion of Canada was created, aside from completing the railroad?

Answers

1. France and Great Britain fought the Seven Years' War. The treaty that ended the war gave New France to Great Britain.

2. Upper Canada was home to mainly English-speaking colonists, and Lower Canada was home to most of the French-speaking colonists.

3. Managing the government of the colonies cost Great Britain money. If the colonies were independent, they would pay for their own governance.

4. If the colonies united as one country, it would only require getting one federal government to agree to build a cross-country railroad.

5. John A. Macdonald became the first prime minister of Canada

6. He purchased land from the Hudson's Bay Company to expand Canada as well as created the Royal Canadian Mounted Police.

Further Information

How can I find out more about the British North America Act?

Most libraries have computers that connect to a database that contains information on books and articles about different subjects. You can input a key word and find material on the person, place, or thing you want to learn more about. The computer will provide you with a list of books in the library that contain information on the subject you searched for. Non-fiction books are arranged numerically, using their call number. Fiction books are organized alphabetically by the author's last name.

Books

Gwyn, Richard J. *John A.: the Man Who Made Us : the Life and times of John A. Macdonald*. Toronto: Random House Canada, 2007.

Gillmor, Don, Pierre Turgeon, and Achille Michaud. *Canada: a People's History*. Toronto: M&S, 2001.

Murray, Jock, and Janet Murray. *Sir Charles Tupper: Fighting Doctor to Father of Confederation*. Markham, Ont.: Associated Medical Services, 1999.

Websites

www.canlii.org/en/ca/const/const1867.html
Entire document of the BNA Act provided by the Canadian Legal Information Institute

http://thecanadianencyclopedia.com/index.cfm?
PgNm=TCE&Params=A1ARTA0004867
Historica-Dominion Institute's website, providing text and images describing John A. Macdonald's life and legacy

Glossary

colonists: people who take part in founding a new land

confederation: a united group of local governments

constitution: the basic beliefs and laws of a nation that establish the powers and duties of the government and guarantee certain rights to the people under its control

dominion: a self-governing nation

federal: a form of government in which power is distributed between a central authority and individual units

federation: a political body formed by uniting smaller bodies

immigration: when people move from one country to live in another

independent: free from the control of another country; self-governing

militia: a body of citizens with some military training who are called to active duty only in an emergency

pamphlet: a short printed publication with no cover or with a paper cover

province: a division of a country that has its own government

rebel: to be against or fight against the authority of one's government

representation by population: a government in which people vote for people who will represent their interests

seized: took possession by force

settlements: newly inhabited places or regions

sovereign: politically independent

tribute: a payment made by one ruler or nation to another to obtain protection

Index

British North America Act 4, 24, 25, 26, 28, 30
Brown, George 4, 22, 23, 25
Cartier, George-Étienne 4, 16, 17
Constitution 4, 12, 15, 17, 19, 23, 24, 25, 27
Dominion of Canada 11, 25, 28, 30
federation 13, 17
France 4, 6, 7
Great Britain 4, 6, 7, 8, 9, 10, 12, 25
Hudson's Bay Company 28, 30

Macdonald, John A. 4, 14, 15, 17, 21, 25, 28, 29, 30
McGee, Thomas D'Arcy 4, 18, 19, 22
New France 6, 7, 8, 9, 11, 30
railroad 4, 16, 17, 19, 21, 29, 30
Royal Canadian Mounted Police 29
Seven Years' War 4, 7, 30
slavery 4, 22
Treaty of Paris 7
Tupper, Charles 4, 20, 21
United States 4, 6, 8, 10, 19, 21, 22
Upper and Lower Canada 8, 9, 13, 14, 16, 30